SPIES AND THEIR GADGETS

SPIES AND SPYING

KATE **WALKER** I ELAINE **ARGAET**

This edition first published in 2004 in the United States of America by Smart Apple Media.

Smart Apple Media
1980 Lookout Drive
North Mankato
Minnesota 56003

Library of Congress Cataloging-in-Publication Data

Walker, Kate.
   Spies and their gadgets / by Kate Walker & Elaine Argaet.
   p. cm — (Spies and spying)

   Includes index.
   Summary: Presents a brief overview of a number of methods and gadgets used by spies from the earliest uses of codes and ciphers to high-tech methods made possible by computers.

   ISBN 1-58340-341-8
   1. Espionage—Equipment and supplies—Juvenile literature. [1. Espionage—Equipment and supplies.]
   I. Argaet, Elaine. II. Title. III. Series.
   UB270.5.W34 2003
   327.12—dc21   2002044622

First Edition
9 8 7 6 5 4 3 2 1

First published in 2003 by
MACMILLAN EDUCATION AUSTRALIA PTY LTD
627 Chapel Street, South Yarra, Australia, 3141

Associated companies and representatives throughout the world.

Copyright © Kate Walker and Elaine Argaet 2003

Edited by Miriana Dasovic
Text and cover design by Marta White
Maps by Pat Kermode, Purple Rabbit Productions
Photo research by Jes Senbergs

Printed in Thailand

Acknowledgements

The author and the publisher are grateful to the following for permission to reproduce copyright material:

Cover photograph: Magnifying glass, courtesy of Getty Images; eye, courtesy of Ingram Royalty Free Image Library; Blackhawk spy plane, courtesy of NASA.

AAP/AFP Photo, pp. 15 (top), 17 (bottom), 24 (left), 25, 27 (top), 30; AKG London/Erich Lessing, p. 5; Arthur Boyd, Australia 1920–1999, *The Mining Town* 1946–7, oil & tempera on composition board, 87.4 x 109.4cm, National Gallery of Australia, p. 27 (bottom); Austral/Topfoto, p. 23 (bottom); Australian Picture Library/Corbis, pp. 4, 13 (bottom), 15 (bottom), 18 (left); Getty Images, pp. 1, 3, 7, 8, 13 (top), 28 (right), 32 (all); Ingram Royalty Free Image Library, p. 1 (eye); Joubert – B.S.I.P/Auscape, p. 29 (bottom); photo p. 28 (left) from *The Master Book of Spies* by Donald McCormick, p. 160; NASA, p. 17 (top); National Air & Space Museum, Smithsonian Institute, p. 19 (top); The Naval Historical Foundation, p. 21; Terry Oakley/The Picture Source, p. 29 (top); Reuters, p. 23 (top); The Trustees of the Imperial War Museum, London, pp. 6, 9 (bottom); Universal Press, p. 27 (map); U.S. Department of Defense, p. 19 (bottom); U.S. Marine Corps, p. 11.

While every care has been taken to trace and acknowledge copyright, the publisher tenders their apologies for any accidental infringement where copyright has proved untraceable. Where the attempt has been unsuccessful, the publisher welcomes information that would redress the situation.

CONTENTS

INTRODUCTION

German soldiers using an Enigma cipher machine in the field.

What is a spy?

A spy is a person who deals in secret information. Some spies gather the information, usually by sly means. Other spies carry the information from one person to another. There are spies who sit at desks and study the information, while other spies go out into the field and act on it. Some spies make up false information and spread it around to fool the enemy. Anyone who works secretly in this way is a spy.

- ◉ The proper name for spying is espionage.
- ◉ The modern name for a spy is an agent or intelligence officer.
- ◉ Information gathered by spies is called intelligence.

When did spying start?

People have been spying on each other since human history began. Army leaders have always known that the best way to defeat an enemy is to find out that enemy's weakness, and the best person to discover that weakness is a spy.

Why do people become spies?

Sometimes people become spies out of loyalty to their country. They gather information that will help keep their country safe. Sometimes people become spies because they know important secret information and sell it for money, usually a lot of money. Some people are tricked or forced into becoming spies. Other people choose to become spies because they find it exciting.

Spy gadgets in early times

For thousands of years, spies used a few simple gadgets. They wrote messages in code or cipher. Sometimes they penned messages in invisible ink or sent messages off by carrier pigeon.

Spies and the age of invention

In the 1800s, many new gadgets were invented. A spy could use a camera to take pictures of the enemy's guns and forts. Any information found could be sent quickly using a radio. Machines were invented that could make up ciphers too complicated for any human brain to work out. When the first planes lifted off the ground in the early 1900s, spies quickly took to the air. Fifty years later, spying moved out into space with the launch of the first satellites.

High-tech spies

Today's spies have hundreds of amazing gadgets that gather information. They have powerful computers that work 24 hours a day, snooping through cyberspace and listening in on mobile telephone calls. Many spies of the future will not be human at all. They will be drones. However, even a drone will need a clever spy at the controls telling it where to go, what to look for, and how to send the information home.

A radio receiver used during World War II, disguised as a set of false teeth.

cipher	a secret language that hides words by jumbling their letters
code	a secret language
cyberspace	the world of computers and the Internet
drones	mobile machines that perform tasks on their own
gadgets	special tools
into the field	going into other countries to spy

THE ENIGMA CIPHER MACHINE

BACKGROUND

? A radio message sent by a spy can be picked up by enemy radio receivers as well.

? However, if that message is sent in cipher, then the enemy can hear the message but not work out what it says.

An Enigma machine.

The Enigma machine

In 1929, a German man named Arthur Scherbius built an amazing cipher machine. He asked mathematicians to try to "crack" the cipher. No one could. When World War II started in 1939, German military intelligence built dozens of these machines. It used them to send top-secret messages. The machine was called Enigma.

How Enigma worked

Enigma was like an electric typewriter. A message was typed onto the keyboard, and a set of wheels inside the machine turned around. As one wheel turned, it then turned another wheel. This caused the letters to be swapped as they were typed in. For example, the letter D might be swapped for the letter F. The letter I might be swapped for Z. D typed in a second time would be swapped for a different letter, such as Y. This would make the word "did" look like "fzy." A whole message typed into an Enigma machine came out looking like a string of meaningless letters. These letters were then sent over the radio using Morse code.

Understanding the message

When the jumbled message was received, it had to be typed into another Enigma machine. The wheels turned and changed the letters back to what they had been. However, the wheels had to be set in exactly the right place before the message was typed in. There were millions of different ways of setting the wheels. The Germans believed that no one could break the Enigma cipher.

How the British cracked the cipher

In 1939, Polish Underground fighters found a set of Enigma wheels and gave them to the British. The British used these wheels to build an Enigma machine of their own. Teams of mathematicians worked day and night trying to crack the cipher. Finally, two months later, they did. The British were able to read the Germans's top-secret messages. This was not always easy. Every day, the Germans set the wheels in a new position. Each day, the British had to work frantically to figure out what this new setting was.

The world's first computer

The first computer in the world was built to work out the daily change of the Enigma wheels. This computer was called Colossus, and it was housed at Bletchley Park in England. Some 7,000 people worked at Bletchley Park deciphering Enigma messages. The work was top secret. Once a person came to work at Bletchley Park, they had to stay there for the rest of the war.

This beautiful old home at Bletchley Park was the secret British cipher school. The first computer in the world, Colossus, was housed here.

deciphering unjumbling the letters of a secret cipher language

mathematicians people who study the science of numbers

Morse code signals of dots and dashes that represent letters of the alphabet

Underground a secret spy force fighting in a country already taken over by the enemy

FOOLING THE ENEMY

Jasper Maskelyne performing a magic trick.

The war in the desert

Major Jasper Maskelyne had been a magician before the war. He joined the British army and trained as a camouflage expert. In 1941, he was sent to work as a backroom boffin in North Africa. The British were trying to safeguard the Suez Canal, a vital shipping lane for British ships.

How Maskelyne hid the Suez Canal

German planes tried to bomb the Suez Canal. They came at night, when British anti-aircraft guns were not as likely to shoot them down. Searchlights along the canal helped the anti-aircraft gunners see the German planes. Maskelyne made the searchlights shine differently. He turned one strong beam of light into many small beams that radiated out like the spokes of a wheel. He also made these lights spin around. This made them appear to flash on and off. German pilots looking down at these flashing lights could not see what was behind them. Maskelyne made the target impossible to see.

Moving Alexandria Harbor

The Germans were also bombing Alexandria Harbor. Maskelyne got an aerial photograph of Alexandria at night so he could see what the lights looked like from the air. He created the same pattern of lights on a beach $1\frac{1}{4}$ miles (2 km) away. When the German bombers came, the lights of Alexandria were turned off and the lights on the beach turned on. The trick worked, and the Germans dropped their bombs on the beach.

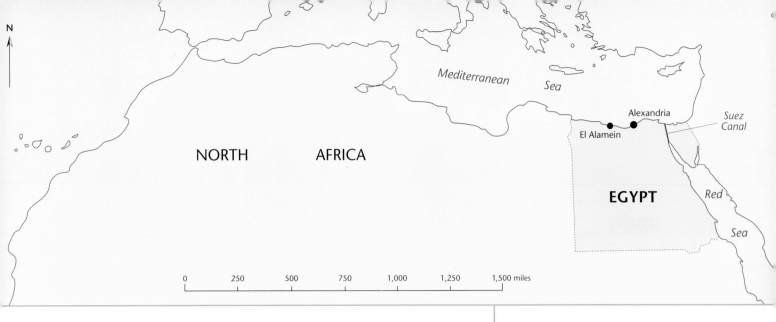

Creating and hiding an army

In 1942, the German and British armies were getting ready for a last great battle in the desert at El Alamein. Germany had the biggest army, and the British were in a bad position. A German minefield lay in front of them. It looked as if the British would have to move part of their army south to give themselves room to fight.

Maskelyne began to build a train out of bulrushes and to lay tin cans to look like railroad tracks heading south. He built dummy tanks of wood and canvas, and thousands of dummy soldiers too. Each day, German planes flew over the British camps and watched the British build this fake railroad line and pretend to move men and equipment south. The trick fooled the Germans into keeping their army divided. Half was in the north and half was in the south.

The real British tanks and guns stayed in the north. Maskelyne made simple wooden covers for these tanks to make them look like ordinary trucks. He also made canvas covers for the guns to make them look like jeeps. British army engineers cleared a path through the minefield. On July 1, 1942, the Germans were taken by surprise when the full force of the British army attacked them from the north. The Germans were utterly defeated.

Dummy tanks are used to fool an enemy.

bulrushes   plants that have strong, straight stems that can be woven together

camouflage   hide an object by making it look like something else

NAVAJO CODE-TALKERS

A great idea

In 1942, Phillip Johnston suggested to the U.S. army that it use Navajo Indians as radio operators in the war in the Pacific. Johnston had lived on a Navajo reservation as a boy. He knew the Navajo language and thought it would make a good code. The Navajo language had never been written down, so the Japanese would not be able to get a copy of it and study it.

Twenty-nine Navajo Indians were given the job of working out a special communication code based on their native language. Some of these recruits were only 15 years old. They had to come up with a list of words most often used by soldiers and commanders in the field. They also had to invent an alphabet so they could spell out any words not on the list. The words had to be short and easy to remember. Also, the Navajo language did not have words for many of the things used by soldiers, such as tanks or submarines. They had to invent words for those.

N

JAPAN

Pacific   Ocean

• Iwo Jima

PAPUA
NEW GUINEA

0   500   1,000   1,500   2,000 miles

Bougainville

Navajo code talk

The Navajos decided not to invent new words. They used ordinary Navajo words in this way:

- *Besh-lo*, which meant "iron fish," was used for submarine.
- *Dah-he-tih-hi*, which meant "hummingbird," was used for fighter plane.
- *Jay-sho*, which meant "buzzard," was used for bomber.
- *Chay-da-gahi*, which meant "tortoise," was used for tank.

The Navajo group studied day and night to memorize the code of 411 words, plus an alphabet. Two U.S. intelligence code-breaking experts tested the code and found it impossible to crack. The experts could not even write down the sounds of the language. The Navajos put on a demonstration for the commanders of the armed forces. The marine commanders were impressed and recruited Navajo Indians into the marines immediately.

In the field

Navajo code-talkers were sent to the most dangerous places in the Pacific. They operated in the front line of battle, and many went behind enemy lines gathering information. During the first two days of the battle of Iwo Jima, six Navajo code-talkers worked constantly, sending and receiving more than 800 radio messages. They did not make a single mistake.

Navajo code-talkers took part in every battle in the Pacific. The Navajo code was so valuable to the U.S. that it was kept secret until 1968. It is the only unbroken code in the history of warfare.

Two Navajo code-talkers send a message from the dense jungle of Bougainville, in Papua New Guinea, close behind the front line of battle.

reservation   land given to Native American Indian peoples to live on

THE SPY WITH THE CAMERA

BACKGROUND

? The camera was invented in 1816.

? Spies have been using cameras as an espionage tool ever since.

John Vassal, the British spy

John Vassal was born in London, England, in 1924. During World War II, he volunteered to become a pilot in the Royal Air Force. He was just 17 years old. The air force did not want Vassal as a pilot, and trained him as a photographer instead. Vassal served with the air force in Europe and found that he liked visiting other countries. When the war ended in 1945, Vassal left the air force and got a job as a clerk with the British navy. This allowed him to work overseas again. Vassal hoped to be sent to Washington, D.C., in the U.S. Instead, in 1954, the navy sent him to Moscow, in the Soviet Union.

Recruited as a spy by the Soviets

Vassal was lonely in Moscow. He was soon targeted by a Soviet agent who made friends with him. This agent convinced Vassal that countries like the U.S. were secretly building weapons and would try to take over the world. The Soviet agent said that the world's only hope for freedom was the Soviet Union. He told Vassal that the Soviets were gathering information to use in a worldwide peace conference. Vassal believed this. When he returned to England in 1956, he became a spy for the Soviets.

UNITED STATES OF AMERICA

Washington, D.C.

Atlantic Ocean

BRITAIN

ENGLAND

London

Moscow

U.S.S.R. (SOVIET UNION)

N

Pacific Ocean

Indian Ocean

0   2,000   4,000   6,000   8,000   10,000 miles

Spying with a camera

Vassal worked in a navy office where secret documents were kept. These documents showed details about British anti-submarine techniques and gunnery trials, orders to the British fleet, and military agreements between Britain and other countries. Each day, Vassal sneaked one of these documents out of the office. In his apartment, he laid the documents on a table and shone a strong light on them. Then he took a photograph of each page using a special camera the Soviets had given him. Vassal did not have to develop the photographs. He would meet his Soviet contact on a street corner in London and hand over the film. Vassal was paid about £600 a year for spying.

Vassal is arrested

By 1962, the navy knew there was a spy in their midst. Special British agents searched the office workers' desks at night. Nothing suspicious was found in Vassal's desk. However, it was learned that he had an expensive apartment and often went on overseas vacations. This meant he had to be earning extra money in some way. On September 12, Vassal's apartment was searched. Agents found two cameras and 140 rolls of film containing photographs of secret navy files. Vassal was arrested and sentenced to 18 years in prison.

Today's spy

Spies today use cameras just as Vassal did. The advantage of the camera is that it takes an exact copy of a document, and the enemy does not know that information has been stolen.

John Vassal, the photographer spy.

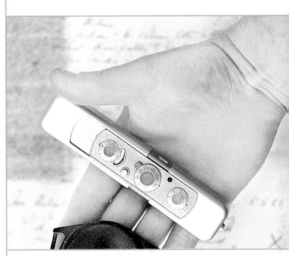
A tiny Minox camera used to secretly photograph documents.

clerk   a person who works in an office filing papers

Soviet Union   a shortened name for the Union of Soviet Socialist Republics (U.S.S.R.), once called Russia

THE DEPARTMENT OF DIRTY TRICKS

Dr. Gottlieb tries to assassinate Fidel Castro

Dr. Sidney Gottlieb was a doctor of chemistry who was born in New York in 1918. He started working for the CIA (Central Intelligence Agency) in 1951.

In 1959, rebel leader Fidel Castro took over the island of Cuba in the Gulf of Mexico. Castro was friendly with the U.S.'s enemy, the Soviet Union. He let the Soviets build missile-launching pads in Cuba. It looked as if Castro was helping the Soviets get ready to launch a nuclear attack against the United States. Sidney Gottlieb offered to assassinate Castro in such a way that no one would know who had done it.

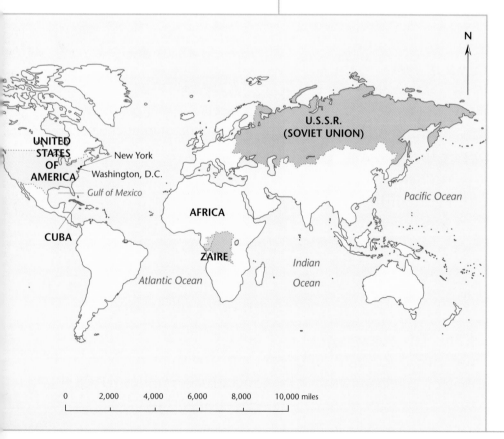

Poison smoke

Fidel Castro liked to smoke cigars, so Gottlieb developed a special poison that could be put into cigars. When the smoker lit the cigar and inhaled, the deadly poison would be drawn into their lungs. The plan was to smuggle these cigars into Castro's home. The poison cigars were made and sent, but mysteriously they never arrived.

More dirty schemes

Castro liked to swim on coral reefs. Gottlieb's next idea was a poison wetsuit. The wetsuit was made and sent, but Castro never put it on. Castro also collected seashells. Gottlieb rigged up a bomb inside a beautiful conch shell. For some reason, the exploding conch shell was never planted.

Dr Sidney Gottlieb (left).

Gottlieb's African visit

In 1960, Gottlieb offered to secretly assassinate another government leader. This time his target was Patrice Lumumba, prime minister of the Congo in Africa. (The Congo was later called Zaire.) Gottlieb spent hours in his laboratory putting together a special poison. It was a mixture of deadly biological germs that included rabbit fever, anthrax, smallpox, and Venezuelan sleeping sickness. These germs were mixed with toothpaste and put into a tube. The plan was to slip the deadly toothpaste into Lumumba's bag while he was traveling. Lumumba did not die of the poison. Gottlieb had forgotten to check whether Lumumba used toothpaste to clean his teeth.

Gottlieb at home

Gottlieb lived on a small farm near Washington, D.C. He did not want his neighbors wondering how he made his living. As a cover, he grew Christmas trees and sold them once a year. He also raised goats. Gottlieb believed that goat's milk was very healthy. He milked his own goats and drank goat's milk all the time.

Cuban leader Fidel Castro liked to smoke big cigars.

assassinating   murdering a person for a political cause

SPY PLANES

BACKGROUND

? Countries spy on each other from high in the sky.

? They use spy planes that fly very fast and take pictures of everything on the ground.

The Blackbird SR–71A

The Blackbird spy plane was built by the U.S. air force in 1968. Blackbirds can fly at an amazing 2,000 miles (3,220 km) per hour. At this speed they cannot be seen by people on the ground, nor do they show up on radar screens. Blackbirds fly at a height of 85,300 feet (26,000 m). Spy planes need to fly high so that the people they are spying on cannot shoot them down. Missiles fired from the ground cannot reach that height.

The spy-plane cameras

When a Blackbird is on a spy mission, its onboard cameras can take clear pictures of objects no larger than a baseball bat. Also, Blackbird cameras take real-time photographs. The instant the photograph is taken, it is beamed to a satellite orbiting (moving around) Earth. The satellite then beams the pictures to a receiving station on the ground. Within a few minutes, people on the ground can see the photographs.

During the war between North Vietnam and South Vietnam, Blackbird spy planes took pictures that showed secret enemy camps and guns hidden deep in the jungle. Blackbirds were used by the U.S. air force for 30 years. No Blackbird was ever shot down.

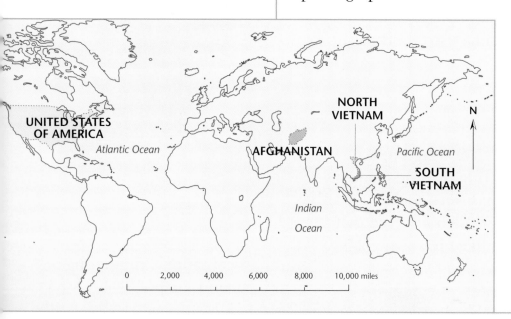

UNITED STATES OF AMERICA

Atlantic Ocean

NORTH VIETNAM

N

AFGHANISTAN

Pacific Ocean

SOUTH VIETNAM

Indian Ocean

0   2,000   4,000   6,000   8,000   10,000 miles

The Global Hawk RQ–4A

Global Hawk is the latest U.S. spy plane. Global Hawks were first used in the "war against terrorism" in Afghanistan in 2001. Global Hawks are unmanned drones. They have no pilot, and take off and land with the help of computers. Global Hawks fly at a speed of 350 miles (570 km) per hour, and cruise at a height of 60,700 feet (18,500 m). Each Global Hawk plane carries enough fuel to keep it in the air for 24 hours. No other spy plane has been able to stay airborne this long. (Blackbird spy planes need to refuel every 45 minutes when they are flying at top speed.)

The Blackbird spy plane is still the fastest plane in the world.

Cameras, infra-red scanners, and radar

Global Hawks are made to circle high above a target and take photographs. They also use infra-red scanners to find and identify objects on the ground. The scanners can find anything made of metal, such as trucks, and anything giving off heat, such as people. Infra-red scanners can find targets at night and even targets hidden underground. Global Hawks also use synthetic aperture radar. This special radar produces images so clear that they look like photographs. Information from the scanners and radar is put together to reveal details that may not appear clearly on a photograph. In the mountains of Afghanistan, Global Hawk spy planes found tiny cave entrances that were missed even by the soldiers on the ground.

The slow-flying Global Hawk spy plane.

SPY SATELLITES

BACKGROUND

? Satellites are unmanned space vehicles that move around Earth in a fixed orbit.

? They carry equipment such as cameras, radar, and antennas for sending and receiving signals.

? The first satellite was launched on October 4, 1957, by the Soviet Union. It was called *Sputnik I*.

A model of the tiny *Sputnik I* satellite.

The first spy satellite

Three months after the launch of *Sputnik I*, the U.S. successfully launched its first satellite, *Explorer I*. However, the world's first spy satellite was not successfully launched until August 19, 1960. It was called *Corona*. It was a U.S. satellite that carried a Key Hole camera that took photographs of the landscape of the Soviet Union and China. After the photographs were taken, a sealed container with the film inside was dropped from the satellite. This container had to be caught mid-air by a plane towing a large net. These first photographs were very fuzzy.

In 1961, the U.S. air force launched its first military intelligence satellite. It was called SAMOS (Satellite and Missile Observation System). Its job was to take pictures of military bases in the Soviet Union, to see if the Soviets were getting ready for war. SAMOS satellites had more advanced Key Hole cameras that could develop the pictures in space and then beam them back to Earth as television images. These first television images showed only large objects, such as airfields. Today's Key Hole cameras can beam back images so sharp that they show details on objects only 6 inches (15 cm) long.

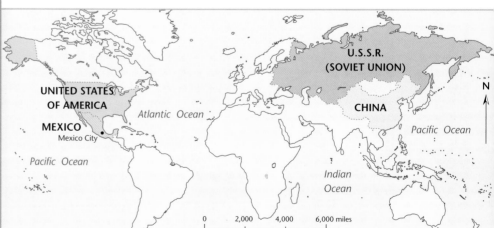

Satellite spies

In April 1975, a young American named Andrew Lee walked into the Soviet embassy in Mexico City and handed a note to the first person he met. The note said he had secrets to sell. The secrets actually came from his friend Christopher Boyce. Boyce worked for the U.S. company that made Key Hole satellites. Boyce took photographs of secret documents. He gave these photographs to Lee, who sold them to the Soviets in Mexico.

One day, Lee got angry at his Soviet contact and threw a book into the embassy grounds. The Soviets thought it was a bomb and called the police. Lee was arrested and sentenced to life imprisonment for spying. Boyce was also caught and sentenced to 40 years in jail.

A plane catching a film container dropped from an early spy satellite.

What today's satellites can do

The MILSTAR (Military Strategic Tactical And Relay) satellites, launched in 1990, have mapped every square inch of Earth's surface. They have taken pictures of military bases. They can tell when a missile is fired anywhere in the world, and give information on the size of the missile and its target seconds after it leaves the ground.

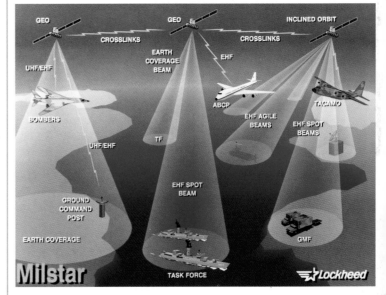

A MILSTAR satellite orbiting Earth.

Killer satellites

Killer satellites orbit Earth ready to knock out enemy space vehicles or other snooping satellites. Killer satellites are small and do not carry explosives. All satellites travel at thousands of miles per hour. A killer satellite only has to crash into another satellite to destroy it.

embassy   building where officials from another country work and sometimes live

SPY SHIPS

The capture of the spy ship USS *Pueblo*

In 1968, the U.S. surveillance ship USS *Pueblo* was on a mission off the coast of North Korea. The *Pueblo* was there to listen to and record signals from North Korean navy ships and coastal stations. On January 23, three North Korean torpedo boats sped towards the *Pueblo*. Two North Korean fighter planes circled overhead.

One of the North Korean ships signaled to the *Pueblo* "Stop or I will open fire." The *Pueblo* signaled back that it was not in North Korea's territorial waters. The *Pueblo* was 16 miles (25.4 km) from the port of Wonsan. The *Pueblo* tried to speed away, so the North Korean torpedo boats fired on it from large guns mounted on their decks. The captain of the *Pueblo* immediately ordered his crew to destroy all the secret information and spy equipment on board. The crew smashed radio and recording equipment with hammers and axes. They burned paper documents in an incinerator. Other files and equipment were thrown overboard.

North Korean sailors armed with machine guns boarded the *Pueblo*. They blindfolded the American crew members, tied their hands, and took them ashore. The crew members were kept in a North Korean prison for 11 months. Finally they were sent home, but the USS *Pueblo* was never returned.

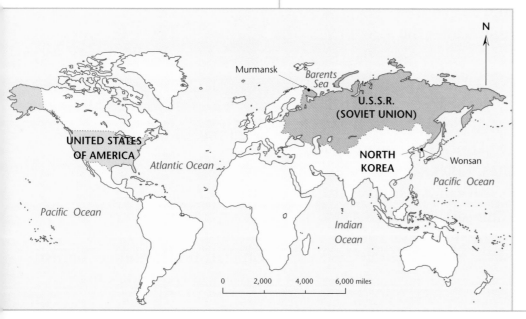

The secret mission of the USS *Parche*

In 1979, the U.S. nuclear submarine USS *Parche* went on a secret mission under the Arctic icecap. It came to rest on the bottom of the Barents Sea, off the north coast of the Soviet Union. Aboard the *Parche* was a group of communications experts. These experts spent all day locked in the submarine's torpedo room, and the submarine crew called them the "spooks."

The spooks were looking for an underwater communications cable that ran between the port of Murmansk and the northern bases of the Soviet naval fleet. They launched a remote-controlled camera from the *Parche*. The camera found the cable, and divers went out and fixed a listening pod to it.

The spooks spent the next two weeks listening to hundreds of different communications lines running through the cable. They chose the ones they wanted, and began recording all the messages sent along those lines. They learned how the Soviets planned to use their navy should there ever be a nuclear war. They also learned that the Soviets did not intend to start a nuclear war by firing nuclear weapons first. This mission was so secret that today the U.S. navy denies that it ever took place.

The USS *Pueblo* showing its many radio antennas.

The USS *Parche* nuclear submarine.

incinerator   a container for burning waste

surveillance   watching and listening

territorial waters   part of the ocean which a country owns because it is close to its coastline

CYBER SPIES

BACKGROUND

? Computers can spy on other computers and also on messages moving through cyberspace.

? Computers can damage or even "kill" other computers.

? Computers and computer operators are the new spies of the 21st century.

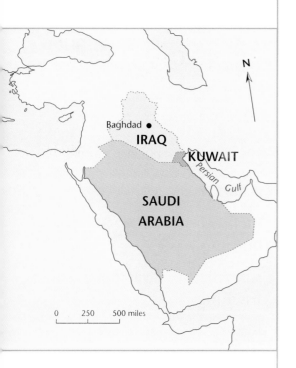

The Gulf War

On August 2, 1990, the president of Iraq, Saddam Hussein, ordered his troops to invade Kuwait. Kuwait is a small country south of Iraq, on the coast of the Persian Gulf. By invading Kuwait, Iraq gained a larger and more secure coastline. The United Nations Security Council ordered President Hussein to withdraw his troops by January 14, 1991. Hussein refused. Two days later, a United Nations taskforce attacked Iraq. The force was led by the U.S. and the conflict was known as the Gulf War.

Cyber warriors in the Gulf War

Long before this war started, U.S. computer experts had been working on ways to attack Iraq secretly. These experts developed a computer virus called AF/91. It was hidden in a computer chip that was built into a printer. In late 1990, U.S. intelligence agents working secretly in Iraq delivered this printer to Iraq's air-defense headquarters in Baghdad. The printer was connected to the air-defense computer, and the virus moved across into that computer. It lay there "asleep" until the war began. Then a special signal was sent to the virus to "wake it up." The virus attacked the computer's memory and shut down Iraq's air-defense system in less than a minute.

An air strike on Iraq during the Gulf War.

Disinformation on the Internet

The Americans used the Internet to spread disinformation during the Gulf War. Disinformation is false information used to fool the enemy. U.S. Internet Web sites reported that Iraq was going to be bombed from the air for a short time, and then tanks and troops would fight the rest of the war on the ground. Iraqi intelligence believed this information and put ground troops in place, ready to begin ground warfare. The information was false. The air strikes continued while Iraqi ground troops waited around with nothing to do.

Internet Web sites also reported that the United Nations planned to land troops along the coast of Kuwait. Large numbers of Iraqi troops were kept busy along the coast getting ready to meet this invasion. This information was also false. The main United Nations invasion force came overland, from Saudi Arabia.

Cyber enemies

Five Dutch computer hackers got into the computers of the U.S. Department of Defense during the Gulf War. They stole important information about the United Nations' troop movements. The hackers also got into the program that supplied the fighting troops with everything from bullets to toothbrushes. They learned how the Americans were using the Internet to send orders back and forth. The hackers offered to sell all this information to Saddam Hussein for $1 million. The U.S. was lucky that Saddam Hussein refused to pay.

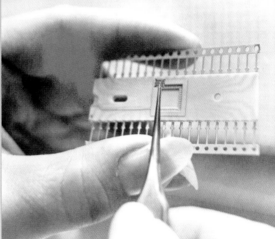
This tiny computer microchip can carry a deadly virus.

computer virus a computer program that damages a computer

hackers computer experts who get into other people's computers without permission

headquarters a central place where information is sent and plans are made

invade use military force to enter someone else's land

United Nations a large group of nations that meet to ensure world peace and fair treatment for all people

THE SPY CRAFT OF ROBERT HANSSEN

BACKGROUND

? Today's spies are highly trained.

? They learn how to follow someone, and how to avoid being followed. They learn how to hand over information without being caught, and much more.

? These skills are called spy craft.

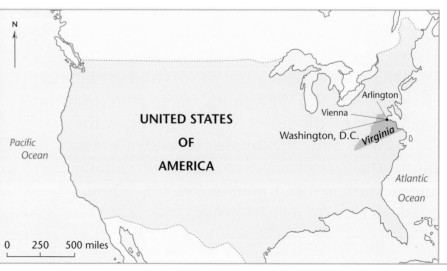

Robert Philip Hanssen.

Hanssen volunteers to spy

Robert Philip Hanssen was an intelligence officer with the FBI (Federal Bureau of Investigation) in the U.S. His job was to catch double agents. In 1985, he became a double agent himself. He sent a letter to the Soviet embassy in Washington, D.C., offering to spy for them. Hanssen was a well-trained officer, and he knew not to give the Soviets his real name. Instead, he used the code name Ramon.

What Hanssen sold the Soviets

For the next 15 years, Hanssen gave the Soviets the names of U.S. spies working as double agents inside the Soviet embassy. Many of these agents were executed. Hanssen gave the Soviets details of different techniques used by the FBI to catch spies. He also revealed many U.S. undercover operations. Hanssen was paid large amounts of cash for this information. He hid most of this money in secret overseas bank accounts. He was also clever enough to have the Soviets pay him in diamonds as well. Diamonds are easy to hide.

N

Pacific
Ocean

UNITED STATES
OF
AMERICA

Arlington

Vienna

Washington, D.C. Virginia

Atlantic
Ocean

0   250   500 miles

The dead-drop site code-named Ellis was a footbridge in a park near Vienna, Virginia.

Hanssen's spy craft

Hanssen never met face-to-face with any Soviet agents. When he had information to sell, he ran a small advertisement in the newspaper. This advertisement had a telephone number and a contact time. The number was always that of a public telephone. Over the telephone, Hanssen arranged two dead drops in Virginia, code-named Ellis and Lewis. He would leave the information at the Ellis site and his contact would leave the payment at the Lewis site. Hanssen also checked FBI computer files regularly to see if he, or any of his dead-drop sites, were being investigated.

Undetected for 15 years

The FBI finally realized that one of its officers was selling information. It got computer experts to search the FBI computers. These experts found that Hanssen had been looking through files he had no need to look through. In Hanssen's own computer, they found an appointment for February 18, 2001, at a park near Vienna, and a second appointment in Arlington. Both of these places were put under surveillance.

Hanssen uses the dead drop

On February 18, 2001, a Sunday, Hanssen drove to the park near Vienna. He placed a package containing secret information under a footbridge. Then he returned to his car. He was shocked when FBI agents appeared and arrested him. The package was retrieved from under the bridge. At the second dead-drop site, FBI agents found another package containing $50,000. Hanssen was charged with espionage, and the Soviets discovered his real name at last.

The $50,000 left for Hanssen at the dead-drop site code-named Lewis.

appointment   a date to meet someone or go somewhere

code name   a simple name used to hide the identity of a spy

dead drops   places where a spy leaves or collects things without meeting another agent

double agents   spies pretending to work for one country while secretly working for another

techniques   special and skilful ways of doing something

HIDING MESSAGES ON THE INTERNET

BACKGROUND

The art of hiding messages is called steganography.

Today's spies send hidden messages over the Internet by hiding them in pictures and in sound recordings.

Internet steganography is called steghide.

How steghide started

Artists and musicians started putting pictures and music on the Internet, expecting that people would like the work and want to buy it. Many people did like the pictures and music, and copied the artist's work into their own computers without paying for it. Worse still, some people made copies of the work and sold it. This happened mostly with music. Some criminals made a lot of money by selling work that did not belong to them.

Experts create electronic fingerprints

Computer experts found a way of putting hidden marks or electronic fingerprints onto pictures and into music files. Anyone seeing the picture on the Internet or hearing the music would not know the fingerprint was there. However, if a copy of the music file was made, the fingerprint would be copied with it. Police could then check the music cassettes or computer disks. If the secret fingerprint was there, hidden in the music, then the work had been copied illegally. The person selling it could be charged with theft.

The Twin Towers of the New York World Trade Center were attacked by al-Qaeda terrorists on September 11, 2001.

Al-Qaeda terrorists used steghide

Spies quickly saw that electronic fingerprinting was a good way to send messages, especially photographs and maps. Osama bin Laden's terrorist group, al-Qaeda, used fingerprinting this way when planning the September 11, 2001, attack on the United States. Al-Qaeda terrorists hid maps and photographs of their targets inside ordinary pictures. They then posted the pictures on sports chat rooms and other Web sites. Thousands of people visited these Web sites and saw nothing suspicious about the pictures. The al-Qaeda spies waiting to receive these pictures knew which ones hid the messages and maps. They downloaded them into their computers and ran them through a fingerprint program. This revealed the images that no one else had seen.

How spies use fingerprinting

Spies who want to send a map over the Internet to another spy first scan the map into their computer. Then they scan a photograph. Next, they use a fingerprint program to embed the image of the map into the photograph. A fingerprint program does not actually lay one image over another. Instead, it hides one image inside the other.

Computers do not see pictures as images. To a computer, a picture is a long list of numbers. Each number is a signal that makes one tiny spot, or pixel, on a computer screen glow with a particular color. The pixels are too small to be seen by the human eye, and it takes millions of glowing pixels to make one picture. This makes it possible for a computer to show us two pictures at once, but for our human eyes to see only one.

A spy would choose a detailed picture to hide a map using a fingerprint program.

illegally   not allowed by law

terrorist   a trained fighter who makes surprise attacks against civilians for a political cause

THE MICRODOT OF THE FUTURE

MIDDLE (OF) DECEMBER AIRPLANE PARTS AND MACHINERY FROM DOUGLAS AND LOCKHEED IN NEW ORLEANS AND GALVESTON ARE TO BE SHIPPED FOR CASABLANCA AND RABAT. THE NAMED FIRMS INTEND TO BUILD THERE ONE ASSEMBLY PLANT EACH IN ORDER TO TAKE UP LATER TOTAL PRODUCTION BY MAKING USE OF AFRICA'S RAW MATERIALS. THE SHIPMENT WILL TAKE PLACE ON FORMER DELTA LINERS. THREE HUNDRED TECHNICIANS OF EACH FIRM ARE GOING ALONG. THE SHIPS WILL BE ATTACHED TO CONVOY. TECHNICAL VANGUARD HAS ALREADY DEPARTED BY WAY OF PAN-AMERICAN AIRLINES. (I) REPEAT THE NAMES: NEW ORLEANS, GALVESTON, DOUGLAS, LOCKHEED, CASABLANCA, RABAT.

A tiny dot of microfilm is enlarged to show the message it carries.

The old microdot

A microdot is a tiny photograph taken of a secret message. The microdot is small enough to paste onto the page of a letter and look like a period. Microdots were used regularly by spies during the Cold War (1945–1989). It is now possible to make microdots that are many thousands of times smaller than this.

A 20th century breakthrough

The great scientific breakthrough at the end of the 20th century was the decoding of human DNA. DNA is a molecule that carries all the information a living cell needs to grow into exactly the sort of cell it should be, such as a skin cell or a blood cell. DNA is an actual message written in a chemical code. The DNA molecule is like two long strands that twist around each other. Between these strands are bars that carry the information coded in chemical "letters." There are three billion chemical letters in a single human DNA molecule. Four chemicals make up this code and scientists have called these four chemicals A, C, G, and T. Scientists have also learned how to engineer or rearrange these codes to improve the way some cells grow. Any kind of code that can be rearranged can be used by spies to send messages.

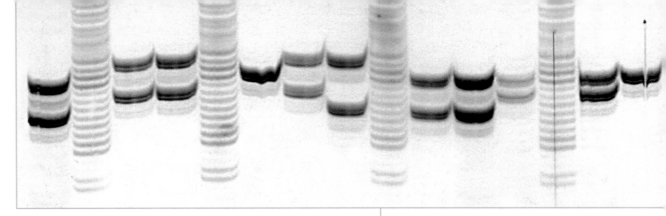

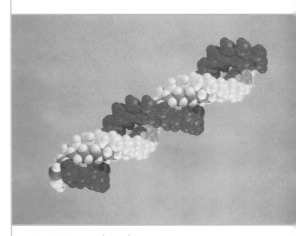
Scientists use computers to print out and read DNA code.

How DNA messages can be sent

There are four chemicals in the DNA code, and these are enough to create a coded alphabet. The A, C, and G chemicals grouped together on one DNA bar could stand for the letter A. The chemicals A, C, and T grouped together could stand for the letter B, and so on. Once a code has been made up for a whole alphabet, a scientist can then take one DNA molecule and rearrange the chemical groups on the bars so they carry a message. Every message would start with a "target" code, just like starting a letter with "Dear Kim."

A DNA molecule.

Sending and receiving DNA messages

The molecule containing the encoded DNA is put into a drop of liquid made up of other human molecules. One drop would contain 30 million molecules, so the message-carrying molecule would be easily hidden among these. The liquid is dropped onto paper and sent as a letter through the mail.

The spy receiving the letter would know where the liquid had been placed and would run that spot of paper through a process called polymerase chain reaction (PCR). This process looks for the "target" code. When it finds the code, it makes thousands of copies of that molecule until that code becomes the main one in the group and is easy to find. Only the spy receiving the message would know the "target" code. Once the molecule is found, the message is easily decoded by a computer.

Cold War   a time of distrust between the world's two superpowers, the U.S. and the Soviet Union, when each thought the other would attack and begin a third world war

molecule   a group of atoms

WHAT IS TO COME?

A Predator drone on a low-flying mission.

The Predator drone

The Predator is an unmanned plane. It is both a spy plane and an attack plane. Predator can take video pictures, infra-red images, and radar images. All these images can be seen immediately by operators on the ground. Predator carries Hellfire anti-tank missiles, which can be fired at an enemy. Predator drones were used in Afghanistan in the "war against terrorism" in 2001 although they were still being tested.

Other flying drones

CamCopters are small, unmanned helicopters. When they are ready for use, they will be able to peek through windows and send back video pictures to base. The U.S. military is also working on a tiny robot bird that will be able to fly though windows and drop "smart dust." This dust is a scattering of hundreds of tiny radio sensors the size of grains of sand. They will send light, heat, and sound readings back to base.

GLOSSARY

appointment   a date to meet someone or go somewhere

assassinating   murdering a person for a political cause

bulrushes   plants that have strong, straight stems that can be woven together

camouflage   hide an object by making it look like something else

cipher   a secret language that hides words by jumbling their letters

clerk   a person who works in an office filing papers

code   a secret language

code name   a simple name used to hide the identity of a spy

Cold War   a time of distrust between the world's two superpowers, the U.S. and the Soviet Union, when each thought the other would attack and begin a third world war

computer virus   a computer program that damages a computer

cyberspace   the world of computers and the Internet

dead drops   places where a spy leaves or collects things without meeting another agent

deciphering   unjumbling the letters of a secret cipher language

double agents   spies pretending to work for one country while secretly working for another

drones   mobile machines that perform tasks on their own

embassy   building where officials from another country work and sometimes live

gadgets   special tools

hackers   computer experts who get into other people's computers without permission

headquarters   a central place where information is sent and plans are made

illegally   not allowed by law

incinerator   a container for burning waste

into the field   going into other countries to spy

invade   use military force to enter someone else's land

mathematicians   people who study the science of numbers

molecule   a group of atoms

Morse code   signals of dots and dashes that represent letters of the alphabet

reservation   land given to Native American Indian peoples to live on

Soviet Union   a shortened name for the Union of Soviet Socialist Republics (U.S.S.R.), once called Russia

surveillance   watching and listening

techniques   special and skilful ways of doing something

territorial waters   part of the ocean which a country owns because it is close to its coastline

terrorist   a trained fighter who makes surprise attacks against civilians for a political cause

Underground   a secret spy force fighting in a country already taken over by the enemy

United Nations   a large group of nations that meet to ensure world peace and fair treatment for all people

INDEX